USING SCIENCE
BE A DEMOLITION EXPERT

By David Dreier

Demolition Consultant: Thomas J. Doud

Series Consultant: Kirk A. Janowiak

ticktock

USING
SCIENCE
BE A DEMOLITION EXPERT

By David Dreier

Consultant: Thomas J. Doud

Series consultant: Kirk A. Janowiak

ticktock project editor: **Joe Harris**

ticktock designer: **James Powell**

With thanks to: Sara Greasley and Hayley Terry

Copyright © ticktock Entertainment Ltd 2008
First published in Great Britain in 2008 by ticktock Media Ltd.,
Unit 2, Orchard Business Centre, North Farm Road, Tunbridge Wells, Kent, TN2 3XF

ISBN 978 1 84696 621 7 pbk
ISBN 978 1 84696 683 5 hbk
Printed in China

DAVID DREIER

David L Dreier (BS Journalism) is a freelance science writer in the United States. He spent much of his career at World Book Publishing in Chicago, Illinois, including six years as Managing Editor of *Science Year*, World Book's science and technology annual. He has also worked as a science reporter for a metropolitan daily newspaper, the *San Antonio [Texas] Express & News*. In addition to writing about science, David has a great interest in history and has written a number of historical articles.

KIRK A. JANOWIAK

BS Biology & Natural Resources, MS Ecology & Animal Behavior, MS Science Education. Kirk has enjoyed teaching students from preschool through to college age. He has been awarded the National Association of Biology Teachers' Outstanding Biology Teacher Award and was honoured to be a finalist for the Presidential Award for Math and Science Teaching. Kirk currently teaches Biology and Environmental Science and enjoys a wide range of interests from music to the art of roasting coffee.

THOMAS J. DOUD

Thomas J Doud III is Project Manager of Explosives Operations at Controlled Demolition Incorporated (CDI). He has worked on a multitude of high-rise office buildings, bridges, chimneys and industrial maintenance blasting projects undertaken by CDI, both in the US and internationally. He began work with CDI as a labourer in 1989, and has since been blaster-in-charge of numerous projects. Thom is a member of the Institute of Explosive Engineers.

▶ CONTENTS

This book supports the teaching of science at Key Stage 2 of the National Curriculum. Students will develop their understanding of these areas of scientific inquiry:

- Ideas and evidence in science
- Investigative skills
- Obtaining and presenting evidence
- Considering and evaluating evidence

Students will also learn about:

- The properties of construction materials
- Gravity and structural integrity
- Mechanical and explosive demolition
- Toxic materials and their effects
- Momentum and impact force
- How hydraulic systems work
- Shearing and crushing forces
- Recycling and reuse of materials
- Protecting people and property from an explosion
- High and low explosives
- What happens in an explosion
- Health and safety in demolition

HOW TO USE THIS BOOK

Science is important in the lives of people everywhere. We use science at home and at school – in fact, all the time. Everybody needs to know about science to understand how the world works. A demolition expert needs to understand physics, chemistry, and biology to bring down buildings – safely and quickly. With this book, you'll use science to plan and complete the demolition of two buildings.

This exciting science book is very easy to use – check out what's inside!

INTRODUCTION

Fun to read information about being a demolition expert.

FACTFILE

Easy to understand information about how demolition works.

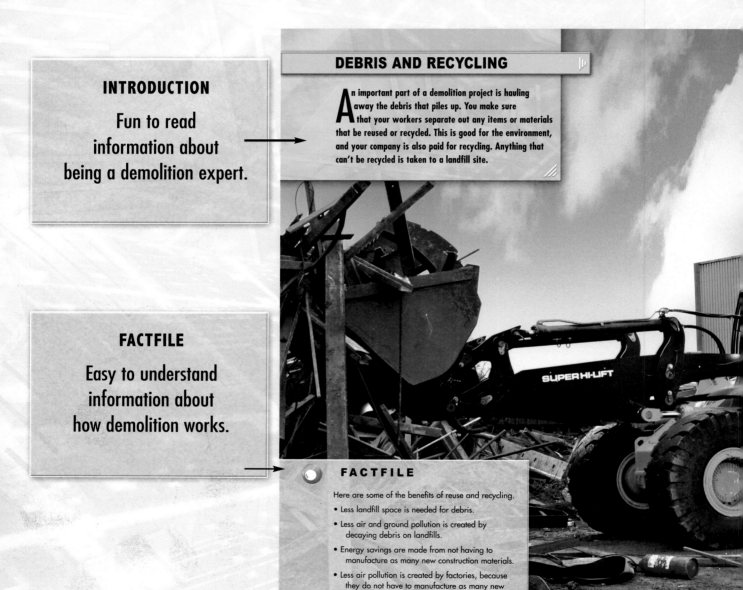

DEBRIS AND RECYCLING

An important part of a demolition project is hauling away the debris that piles up. You make sure that your workers separate out any items or materials that be reused or recycled. This is good for the environment, and your company is also paid for recycling. Anything that can't be recycled is taken to a landfill site.

FACTFILE

Here are some of the benefits of reuse and recycling.

- Less landfill space is needed for debris.
- Less air and ground pollution is created by decaying debris on landfills.
- Energy savings are made from not having to manufacture as many new construction materials.
- Less air pollution is created by factories, because they do not have to manufacture as many new construction materials.

WORKSTATION

Real-life demolition experiences, situations and problems for you to read about.

CHALLENGE QUESTIONS

Now that you understand the science, put it into practice.

WORKSTATION

This pie chart shows how much of each material is found in demolition debris.

Material	
Wood	
Concrete, bricks, asphalt	
Drywall (plaster & wood pulp)	
Roofing	
Other	
Rebar and other metals	

Pie chart: $\frac{1}{12}$, $\frac{1}{4}$, $\frac{1}{6}$, $\frac{1}{8}$, $\frac{1}{8}$, $\frac{1}{4}$

What happens to demolition debris?

- Useful items such as doors and sinks are almost always saved and resold.
- Wood is often reused in construction, and as wood chips.
- Bricks are cleaned for reuse in new buildings.
- Concrete is ground up and used under the tarmac of new roads.
- Rebar and other metals are melted and recycled into new metal items.

How much of demolition debris is recycled?

- In the United States, only about $\frac{1}{4}$ (one quarter) of the debris from demolition sites is recycled. The rest goes to landfills.
- In England, about $\frac{1}{2}$ (one half) of debris from demolition sites is recycled.
- However, it is estimated that $\frac{3}{4}$ (three quarters) of the debris from demolition could be reused or recycled.

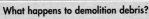

Q CHALLENGE QUESTIONS

1. What proportion of demolition debris could be recycled to create new metal items?
2. How does recycling demolition debris help to reduce air pollution?
3. Which two kinds of materials make up one half of demolition debris?
4. Which material from demolition is used for building new roads?

19

IF YOU NEED HELP!

TIPS FOR SCIENCE SUCCESS

On page 30 you will find lots of tips to help you with your science work.

ANSWERS

Turn to page 31 to check your answers. (*Try all the activities and questions before you take a look at the answers.*)

GLOSSARY

On page 32 there is a glossary of demolition and science words.

WHAT GOES UP...

You're a demolition engineer, and you've just been given your first big project. You have been asked to demolish two buildings: a 15-storey steel-frame office building, and a 18-storey reinforced-concrete block of flats. You have learned all your demolition skills on the job. That's the only way – there are no schools where you can receive training as a demolition engineer. Now you're ready to test those skills. So let's get to it!

FACTFILE

There are various reasons for demolishing buildings and other structures.

- Some are old and in danger of collapsing without warning.
- Others have been damaged by a fire or an earthquake and are beyond repair.
- And some are simply no longer useful.

Before you can think about demolishing buildings, you need to understand how they have been built. Most large buildings are constructed of either steel or reinforced concrete.

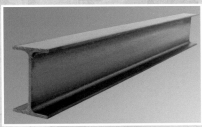

A steel girder.

Steel-reinforced concrete.

STEEL BUILDINGS

- The 15-storey office building is a steel building.
- Steel buildings are made from heavy steel girders bolted or welded together. Concrete is poured at the base of each storey to make the floor surface. The outer covering of the building is usually glass.
- The girders supporting the building are hidden inside it. Because the outer walls do not bear the weight of the building, they are called curtain walls.

REINFORCED CONCRETE BUILDINGS

- The block of flats is made of reinforced concrete.
- Reinforced concrete contains steel rods, known as rebar (short for reinforcing bars). Rebar greatly strengthens a concrete structure.
- Liquid concrete is poured around rebar when a building is being constructed, and it hardens around the rods.

The force of gravity pulls objects towards the centre of the Earth. Any object will fall down due to the force of gravity unless something stands up against that force.

- The strong columns of a building provide a balancing force opposing that of gravity. This is called structural integrity.
- A building stands securely because it has balanced forces. As long as gravity is balanced by structural integrity, a building will not fall.
- Demolition engineers may intentionally weaken the columns of buildings with explosives. This allows them to use gravity to tear down the building.

GRAVITY

STRUCTURAL INTEGRITY

Q CHALLENGE QUESTIONS

1. Give three reasons why the office building and block of flats might need to be destroyed.
2. What is the force that stops tall buildings from collapsing due to gravity?
3. How do demolition engineers sometimes use gravity to destroy buildings?
4. How can a concrete wall be made stronger?

THE CHALLENGE

You've arrived at the demolition site of the 15-storey steel-frame office building. You and your team make a careful inspection of a building, inside and out. You must decide exactly how to proceed with the demolition. The first thing you need to decide is whether to use mechanical methods or explosives. Mechanical demolition uses large machines to cut, crush or knock down buildings. Explosive demolition uses controlled blasting to make buildings implode.

Demolition engineers must gather as much information as they can about a building. They will look at its blueprints, and use special instruments to record information about the building.

FACTFILE

Implosion can mean two different things.

- In science, the word implosion means an inward collapse caused by outside pressure, such as air or water pressure.
- In demolition, a building implosion is a vertical collapse caused by gravity.

Most buildings are demolished with mechanical methods.

- For buildings up to about 15 storeys high, mechanical methods are usually the best choice.

- If a building is very close to other buildings, explosives may cause damage to the other buildings. In this case, mechanical methods may also be the best choice.

Only about one building in 100 is destroyed with explosives.

- With buildings of more than 15 storeys, however, it gets more difficult for machines to reach the upper storeys. Explosives may then be the best option.

- If there is little or no room for wrecking machines to move around the building, then explosives may be the only option.

- But there is no set rule for when explosives are used. Sometimes, buildings as low as eight storeys are brought down with explosives. This is because explosive demolition is quicker than mechanical demolition.

Q CHALLENGE QUESTIONS

1. Do you think you should use mechanical or explosive demolition on your buildings?

   A. The office building is 15 storeys high, and it stands very close to an old church on one side and a library on the other. It is, however, possible to access it from the front and back.

   B. There is very little space for demolition vehicles to move around the block of flats, which is 18 storeys high.

2. Construction of a new building needs to start very soon on the site of the building you are demolishing. What kind of demolition might you use to get the job done as quickly as possible?

TOXIC MATERIALS

Work has begun on the two buildings. Under your instruction, the demolition team has started 'soft strip' inside the office building. This is the removal of doors, windows, and other things that are not part of the structure that supports the building. Workers wearing protective clothing take out objects containing harmful materials. This work will go on for several weeks before demolition can begin.

The workers soft stripping this building wear face masks to keep them from breathing in toxic materials.

FACTFILE

- Buildings constructed before the 1970s often contain toxic materials.
- These includes asbestos, mercury, lead, and PCBs (polychlorinated biphenyls).
- If you breathe in asbestos, it can stay in your body for years, because it doesn't break down. It can cause health problems many years later.

WORKSTATION

Before a building can be demolished, you must give it a complete inspection for harmful waste.

- Harmful materials must be very carefully removed and disposed of.
- If a building was demolished without first removing these dangerous materials, the collapse of the building would create a toxic cloud that could harm people who live or work nearby.

This chart lists the most common hazardous materials removed from older buildings, what they are used for, and some of their effects.

This symbol is used to warn people that a material is toxic.

TOXIC MATERIALS

	Material	Used in	Effects
	Asbestos	Insulation materials	Scarring of the lungs, and lung cancer
	Lead	Paints, pipes	Blood diseases; kidney damage; nerve and brain damage
	Mercury	Paints	Skin disorders; rashes; kidney damage; nerve damage
	PCBs	Electrical equipment	Skin, nose, and lung irritations; cancer

Q CHALLENGE QUESTIONS

1. If a worker has been removing paint from the walls of old buildings and develops a blood disease, what do you think may have happened?

2. Which harmful material might cause someone to become ill many years after a demolition job? Why is this?

3. If a worker suffered from breathing problems, what might they have been exposed to?

4. A person who develops a skin rash and nerve problems may have been exposed to what toxic substance?

WRECKING BALL

Now that the office building is completely safe, you can begin demolition. You have decided to knock down the top floors with a wrecking ball – a huge iron weight suspended on a cable from a tall crane. Operating a wrecking ball requires great skill, and your operator is one of the best in the business. As the wrecking ball delivers crushing blows to the top of the building, debris falls from the upper storeys onto the ground.

 FACTFILE

Wrecking balls can weigh between two and five tons.

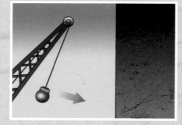

When the wrecking ball is released, it is pulled downwards by gravity. As it moves down, the chain pulls it forwards.

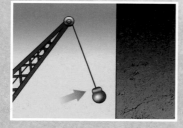

It continues to swing forwards and upwards because it is carried onwards by its own weight and speed. This is called its momentum.

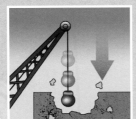

A wrecking ball can be either swung into the side of building or dropped down onto it.

- Even a motionless wrecking ball exerts a downward force because of gravity. That force is equal to its weight.

- When a wrecking ball is dropped onto a flat surface – or swung into a wall – the amount of force it exerts increases greatly.

- Gravity causes the ball to accelerate, or gain speed. Because the ball is travelling so fast, it has a huge impact force when it smashes into something. That force is measured in pounds.

- The further an object falls, the more it accelerates and the greater the force.

The impact force of a wrecking ball is measured in newtons. This graph shows the massive impact force produced by a two-ton wrecking ball as it is dropped from different heights.

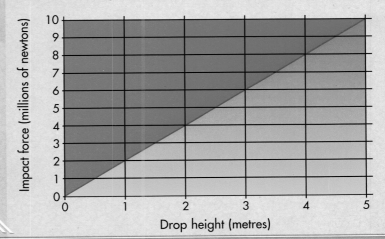

Q CHALLENGE QUESTIONS

1. How much impact force does a two-ton wrecking ball have when dropped from a height of three metres?

2. From what height would a two-ton wrecking ball have to be dropped for it to have an impact force of about eight million newtons?

3. How much downward force would a motionless five-ton wrecking ball have?

4. Which force causes a wrecking ball to accelerate downward?

5. Wrecking balls are made of iron or steel rather than wood or plastic. Why do you think this is?

HYDRAULIC EXCAVATORS

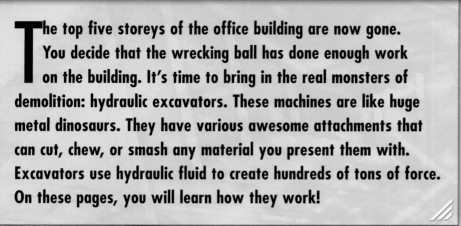

The top five storeys of the office building are now gone. You decide that the wrecking ball has done enough work on the building. It's time to bring in the real monsters of demolition: hydraulic excavators. These machines are like huge metal dinosaurs. They have various awesome attachments that can cut, chew, or smash any material you present them with. Excavators use hydraulic fluid to create hundreds of tons of force. On these pages, you will learn how they work!

FACTFILE

When you push on something, you are adding a force to the object. This force creates pressure. Putting pressure on the surface of a liquid, like water, makes the water try to move away from the pressure. If the water is in a tube (or a cylinder) and you push the water on one end of the tube, the water will want to move toward the other end of the tube.

WORKSTATION

A piston is a tube with a tight-fitting plug, which can move in or out.

- If you push a piston into a tube filled with a fluid, the fluid moves away from the piston. The pressure of the push can be measured in kilograms.

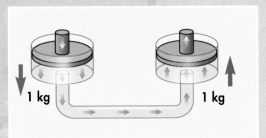

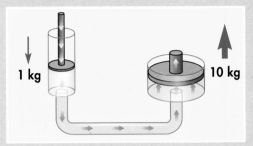

- The two pistons in this picture (above) have the same surface area. Surface area means the surface on which the fluid can push.
- If you push one piston down with a force of one kilogram, an upward force of one kilogram will push against the other piston. The pistons will move the same distance.

- In this second example, the piston on the right has ten times the surface area of the piston on the left.
- If you apply a downward force to the left piston, a force **ten times greater** will push against the right piston. But the piston on the right will only move **one tenth** of the distance of the piston on the left.

Fluid moving through the tubes to create a change in pressure is 'hydraulics'.

- Hydraulic systems move things by applying pressure to fluid in a tube or cylinder. This is how the excavator's arm moves.
- A small force is applied to the fluid in the narrow tubes on the arm.
- This force is transferred to the larger cylinder that is bolted to the arm.
- The force of the piston in the large cylinder moves the large, strong arm of the excavator.
- Hydraulic excavators use cylinders of different sizes to increase the force they apply.

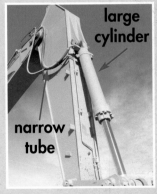

large cylinder

narrow tube

Q CHALLENGE QUESTIONS

Piston B has a surface area ten times larger than Piston A.

1. How far will Piston A have to move for Piston B to move three centimetres?

2. If Piston A is pushed down with a force of four kilograms, how much upwards force will apply to Piston B?

3. If Piston A is pushed down five centimetres, how far will Piston B rise?

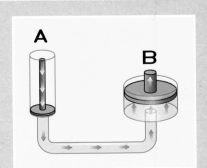

OPERATING AN EXCAVATOR

Y ou've learned how to operate an excavator, so you can take the controls of one of these machines. It's a big yellow monster fitted with a powerful fast-moving hammer called a hydraulic breaker. You operate the excavator with a pair of joysticks and two foot pedals. You pull one of the joysticks back to raise the excavator's arm. Then, by pressing a button on the stick, you start the hydraulic breaker. You watch as it smashes through the concrete walls of the building.

This is the hydraulic breaker.

The joysticks are used to swing the excavator's cab around, to control the boom – the long jointed arm – and to operate the breaker.

You move the excavator on its tracks using the foot pedals or levers.

WORKSTATION

There are excavator attachments for every demolition task you can think of. Among the attachments commonly used on demolition projects are:

Shears: giant cutting mechanisms that can cut through almost anything, including steel beams six inches thick.

Hydraulic breakers: these pound apart stone or concrete surfaces using hard chisel-like impacts.

Grapple jaws: for grasping and moving heavy objects.

Pulverisers: for crushing and dismantling low walls and floors.

scissors = small surface area

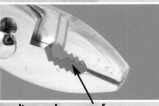
pliers = large surface area

Some excavator attachments exert a shearing force, while others exert a crushing force.

- Shears act like giant scissors. They exert a great deal of force along a narrow line, enabling them to cut cleanly through thick metal or other materials.

- Pulverisers are similar to pliers. Their force is spread across a wider surface, so that a material is crushed and ground into pieces rather than sliced apart.

Q CHALLENGE QUESTIONS

1. Which attachment would you use to smash apart a pavement?
2. If you needed to transport large rocks at a site and pile them up, which attachment would you use?
3. What would be your best choice for cutting through heavy metal pipes?
4. Which two attachments would both be good for demolishing concrete floors in a building?
5. If a tool applies force to a large surface area, is it best for crushing, or cutting?

17

DEBRIS AND RECYCLING

An important part of a demolition project is hauling away the debris that piles up. You make sure that your workers separate out any items or materials that be reused or recycled. This is good for the environment, and your company is also paid for recycling. Anything that can't be recycled is taken to a landfill site.

FACTFILE

Here are some of the benefits of reuse and recycling.

• Less landfill space is needed for debris.

• Less air and ground pollution is created by decaying debris on landfills.

• Energy savings are made from not having to manufacture as many new construction materials.

• Less air pollution is created by factories, because they do not have to manufacture as many new construction materials.

This pie chart shows how much of each material is found in demolition debris.

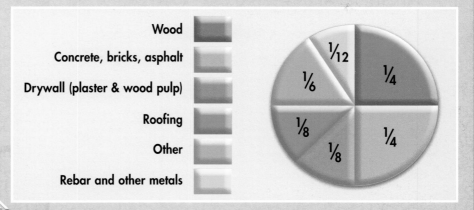

Wood

Concrete, bricks, asphalt

Drywall (plaster & wood pulp)

Roofing

Other

Rebar and other metals

$\frac{1}{12}$ $\frac{1}{4}$ $\frac{1}{6}$ $\frac{1}{8}$ $\frac{1}{8}$ $\frac{1}{4}$

What happens to demolition debris?

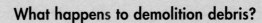

- Useful items such as doors and sinks are almost always saved and resold.
- Wood is often reused in construction, and as wood chips.
- Bricks are cleaned for reuse in new buildings.
- Concrete is ground up and used under the tarmac of new roads.
- Rebar and other metals are melted and recycled into new metal items.

How much of demolition debris is recycled?

- In the United States, only about ¼ (one quarter) of the debris from demolition sites is recycled. The rest goes to landfills.
- In England, about ½ (one half) of debris from demolition sites is recycled.
- However, it is estimated that ¾ (three quarters) of the debris from demolition could be reused or recycled.

Q CHALLENGE QUESTIONS

1. What proportion of demolition debris could be recycled to create new metal items?
2. How does recycling demolition debris help to reduce air pollution?
3. Which two kinds of materials make up one half of demolition debris?
4. Which material from demolition is used for building new roads?

PLANNING AN EXPLOSION

While the demolition of the office building proceeds, you begin to plan how you will demolish the block of flats using explosives. The block of flats has other buildings around it, so you must make sure that it falls straight down and does not tilt to one side. The aim is to just weaken the structure and let gravity do the rest – let the building collapse under its own weight. If this is done correctly, the building will fall in the right direction.

Safety is a incredibly important at a demolition site. Workers are required to wear hard hats and reflective jackets.

WORKSTATION

When a building is imploded, it is often best to have it fall within its footprint.

- A building's footprint is the area it occupies on the ground.
- The Kingdome Stadium in Seattle, USA (shown on the left) fell almost perfectly within its footprint when it was imploded in March 2000.
- All implosions involve a number of explosions, which take place in a planned sequence. But the entire process usually takes less than 30 seconds.

By detonating explosives in a planned order, you can control how a building falls.

- To make a building fall in a particular direction, you detonate explosives at the bottom of that side first. This weakens the building's supports. The building leans in the direction you want. Other explosions throughout the building will bring the whole structure down in that direction.
- To make a building fall inwards, you need to detonate explosives in the middle of the building first, so that the outside walls fall inwards.
- The last explosives to be detonated are usually those on the upper floors of the building. This makes sure that the building collapses in a controlled way.

Q

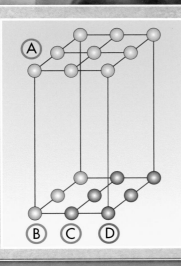

CHALLENGE QUESTIONS

1. In which direction will gravity cause this building to fall if you detonate the explosions in this order: D, C+B, A?

2. If you wanted the building to fall into an empty plot of land to the left, in which order would you detonate the explosives?

3. If there are buildings to both the left and right, in which order would you need to detonate the explosives?

4. If a building to be imploded has other buildings around it on its north, west, and south sides, where should the first explosions occur inside the building?

PLACING EXPLOSIVES

You help the demolition crew as they prepare the block of flats for the implosion. First you use sledgehammers to knock down the non-supporting walls in the building, so that the building can collapse properly. Then you supervise as the crew drill holes in the building's supporting columns and walls, and place sticks of dynamite in them.

After planting explosives in the building's columns, you wrap them in material to contain the flying debris.

FACTFILE

There are two main kinds of explosives.

- **High explosives**, like dynamite, explode with enough force to destroy the supports of buildings. However, it is difficult to ignite a high explosive.

- **Low explosives** burn less quickly but are easier to ignite, so they are often used to help ignite high explosives.

WORKSTATION

When planning an implosion, you do test blasts on columns in the building. This helps you to know how much dynamite you will need to demolish the building.

Columns are wrapped in heavy fabrics before the test blast, to hold in the debris during the explosion.

This column was blown up with too little dynamite.

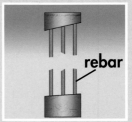

rebar

This column was destroyed with the correct amount of explosives.

TOOLS OF A BLASTER

Blasting machine
By pressing a button on this device, you can send an electrical charge which sets off a single explosive cap, called the firer.

Detonating cords
The firer ignites cords which are filled with an explosive. An explosion travels down each cord and triggers the blasting caps.

Blasting caps
These low explosives are used to ignite larger explosives, such as sticks of dynamite.

High explosives
Concrete can be shattered by dynamite, but for steel columns you must use more powerful high explosives such as RDX.

Q CHALLENGE QUESTIONS

1. Why is it necessary to wrap concrete columns with heavy materials for a test blast?
2. What kind of explosives would you use to implode a steel-frame building?
3. What do you think will happen to the building if you use too much explosive? What if you use too little?
4. High explosives such as dynamite do not ignite easily, but low explosives like blasting caps do. Why are both used together in demolition?

PROTECTING THE PUBLIC

You are now four months into the project. In the block of flats, the crew is making final preparations for the implosion, which is scheduled for later today. You walk through the building to make one last inspection — everything looks good. There's a feeling of excitement in the air. The streets around the building have been cleared of people. But crowds are gathering at the edge of the safety perimeter to watch.

FACTFILE

You have taken steps to protect nearby houses and underground water, gas, and telephone lines.

- The nearby houses have been draped with material to protect them from flying debris and dust.

- The gas and water lines near the building have been covered with large mounds of soil. This is to cushion them from the impact of debris hitting the ground.

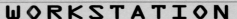

WORKSTATION

ROAD CLOSED

Human safety and protecting property are important to you as you prepare for the implosion.

- With the help of the police and security guards, you move everyone out of the area for a distance of several hundred metres. The police have closed all the surrounding streets to traffic.

FAMOUS IMPLOSIONS OF THE PAST

The amount of explosive needed to destroy a building depends on its height, depth and width, and its construction material.

Building and Location	Year demolished	Height	Construction material	Pounds of explosives used
J L Hudson Department Store, Detroit, USA	1998	21 storeys	Steel	2,728
Mendes Caldeira Building, Sao Paolo, Brazil	1975	32 storeys	Reinforced concrete	1,000
Biltmore Hotel, Oklahoma City, Oklahoma, USA	1977	28 storeys	Steel	800
Philips Building, Oslo, Norway	2000	15 storeys	Reinforced concrete	220

Q CHALLENGE QUESTIONS

1. Look at the chart. Is it true to say that a taller building always requires more explosives than a smaller building? Explain your answer.

2. The J L Hudson store had fewer storeys than the Mendes Caldeira Building, but nearly three times the amount of explosives were needed to implode it. Based on the table above, can you say why this might be?

3. Why are houses draped in material before the implosion?

A REAL BLAST!

The time has arrived for the implosion of the block of flats. A final check has made sure that no one is inside the danger zone. At the barriers, the crowds watch silently. You and your crew have retreated to a safe distance, and now a countdown begins: ten, nine, eight... When the count reaches zero, the blaster turns a switch on the blasting machine. Immediately, there are a number of sharp pops as the detonating cords ignite. Those sounds are followed by loud booms, like fireworks, as the dynamite explodes. The building shudders, and then it crashes to the ground in a huge cloud of dust. A perfect job!

WORKSTATION

What happens in an explosion?

- An explosion is a form of combustion, or burning.
- Combustion is a chemical reaction in which a material combines with oxygen. It gives off energy in the form of heat and light, and releases gases.
- Combustion can happen at different rates. There is a huge difference between the slow rate of combustion of a log in a fireplace and the very fast rate of combustion of an explosive material such as dynamite.

A log in a fireplace may take an hour or more to combust. It releases energy and gases slowly.

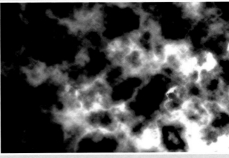

A stick of dynamite combusts within a fraction of a second. In that instant, it releases a great amount of energy and gas.

shock wave   expanding gas

heat and light   pressure

The gas released by an explosive such as dynamite expands rapidly.

- This explosion produces a shock wave that exerts a tremendous amount of pressure on surrounding objects.
- This tremendous pressure causes the most damage in an explosion. It can knock down or tear apart objects nearby. Concrete may shatter, and steel can be torn apart by this kind of force.

Q CHALLENGE QUESTIONS

1. What gas does a combustion need?
2. What kinds of energy are released during combustion?
3. What do we call a very fast rate of combustion?
4. What causes the most damage to objects when an explosion happens: light, heat, or pressure?

WRAPPING IT UP

The dust is settling in the area around the imploded block of flats. All that remains of the building is a eight-metre-high pile of debris. Tomorrow you will put excavators with concrete-pulverizing jaws to work on the rubble. They will break the concrete into small pieces and remove the rebar for recycling. The concrete will be sold to a construction company that builds roads. Everything has worked out well. Best of all, no one was hurt, or suffered from breathing in dust. You'll be back on the job tomorrow, but for now everyone has earned a good night's rest.

FACTFILE

- A major health hazard from demolition is dust, which can cause a number of health problems.
- During a mechanical demolition project, workers often use fire hoses to wet down debris.
- The water keeps dust to a minimum by turning it to mud. This protects both workers and onlookers from breathing it in.

It is almost impossible to prevent a huge cloud of dust from an implosion.

- When the building collapses, air in the building forced out in a great blast of wind. That wind carries a huge amount of dust with it.

- Dust from concrete and bricks contains a substance called silica. Silica can harm the lungs, even if breathed in for only a short time.

- Workers can protect themselves by wearing face masks, which have a fine mesh in them. This mesh lets through air, but pieces of silica are too large to get through.

After the implosion, you must make sure that the site is safe before anyone returns to it.

- You watch videos showing the implosion of the building from several angles.

- You compare the videos to your plans. Did all of the explosives in the building detonate?

- Any explosives that did not detonate must be removed by experts. If they are not removed, they could detonate unexpectedly and injure or kill someone.

- You must check that the building has fully collapsed, and that there is no danger of any further collapse.

Q CHALLENGE QUESTIONS

1. How does hosing a building keep dust to a minimum?

2. How do workers at demolition sites protect themselves from dust?

3. Why is it important to watch the explosion of a building from all angles on video? How does this protect the public?

4. What do you think is the best way protect people watching the implosion from the dust?

TIPS FOR SCIENCE SUCCESS

Pages 10-11

Toxic Materials

Demolition workers aren't the only people who are sometimes exposed to dangerous substances. People who live in old houses can be surrounded by the same sorts of dangers. For example, lead-based paint was very widely used in past decades. When stripping very old paint from house walls, people should find out what kind of paint it is. If it contains lead, they need to wear a protective face mask when they strip the walls.

Pages 12-13

Wrecking Ball

Because weight is a type of force, you are exerting a downward force every time you stand on something. If a bathroom scale says you weigh 45 kilograms, that means you are exerting 45 kilograms of downward force on the scale.

Pages 14-15

Hydraulic Excavators

A fluid is any substance that has no fixed shape and flows easily. Both gases and liquids are fluids. However, the fluids used in hydraulic devices are all liquids. Unlike gases, liquids cannot be compressed. With a gas, pressure simply causes the gas to take up a smaller space. But when you put pressure on a liquid, that pressure is transferred throughout the liquid.

Pages 24-25

Protecting the Public

There is no simple formula for the amount of explosives needed for a building implosion. It depends on three main factors:

- The height of the building
- The width and depth of the building. A short building can still be very wide!
- The kinds of materials it is made of – is it built with steel, or reinforced concrete?

Pages 28-29

Wrapping It Up

Very fine dust is dangerous because it can be breathed far into the lungs, where it stays lodged. Silica in dust can cause a disease called silicosis. It causes the formation of scar tissue in the lungs, which makes it hard to breathe. There is no cure for silicosis.

ANSWERS

Pages 6-7

1. They may be old or in danger of collapsing; they could have been damaged by a fire or earthquake; or they could just be no longer useful.
2. Buildings are kept from collapsing by their structural integrity.
3. Engineers weaken the columns of buildings, so that the building is pulled down by gravity.
4. Rebar (reinforcing bars) would make a concrete wall much stronger.

Pages 8-9

1A. Mechanical demolition.
1B. Explosive demolition.
2. Explosive demolition, because it takes less time than mechanical demolition.

Pages 10-11

1. They might have become sick because of lead in the paint.
2. Asbestos, because it doesn't break down, and can stay in the body for years.
3. Asbestos or PCBs (polychlorinated biphenyls).
4. Mercury.

Pages 12-13

1. Six million newtons.
2. 4 metres.
3. 5 tons.
4. Gravity.
5. Iron and steel are heavy and hard.

Pages 14-15

1. 30 centimetres.
2. 40 kilograms.
3. 0.5 centimetres.

Pages 16-17

1. A hydraulic breaker.
2. Grapple jaws.
3. Shears.
4. The breaker and pulveriser.
5. Crushing.

Pages 18-19

1. 1/12
2. Less air pollution is created by decaying debris, and less is produced by factories because they do not have to manufacture as many new construction materials.
3. Wood, and concrete, bricks and asphalt.
4. Concrete.

Pages 20-21

1. The building would fall to the right.
2. B, C+D, A.
3. You would detonate explosives C first.
4. The first explosions should happen on the east side.

Pages 22-23

1. To contain flying debris that might hurt someone.
2. Powerful explosives such as RDX.
3. If you use too much explosive, flying debris may cause damage to nearby buildings. If not enough explosive is used, the building may not collapse.
4. Low explosives like blasting caps are used to ignite high explosives such as dynamite.

Pages 24-25

1. No, it's not true. The Mendes Caldeira Building required less explosives than the L Hudson Department Store, although it was taller.
2. The L Hudson Department Store was steel, which usually requires more explosives than concrete.
3. To protect them from flying debris.

Pages 26-27

1. Oxygen.
2. Light and heat.
3. An explosion.
4. Pressure.

Pages 28-29

1. Wet dust becomes mud which doesn't float in the air, and so cannot be breathed in.
2. By wearing a protective mask over the mouth and nose.
3. You need to make sure that all the explosives have detonated. If you don't do this, there is a danger that there could be explosives in the rubble, which could detonate without warning and hurt people.
4. Keeping them far away from the site.

CHISEL A tool with a sharp edge, which is struck with a hammer. It is used to chip pieces out of a hard material like stone.

DEBRIS The remains of something that has been destroyed.

DECAY To rot and break down over time.

DETONATE To make something explode.

EXPLOSION A sudden and violent chemical reaction in which heat, light and pressure are released.

FLUID A substance that has no fixed shape and flows easily. Gases and liquids are both fluids.

GIRDER A long metal beam that is used to support a building.

HIGH EXPLOSIVES Explosives, such as dynamite and RDX, that ignite very quickly.

HYDRAULIC FLUID An oil used in hydraulic machinery, such as demolition excavators.

HYDRAULICS A way of multiplying pressure by forcing a liquid through tubes of different sizes. This pressure can be used to move mechanical vehicles.

IGNITE To catch fire or explode.

IMPACT FORCE The force exerted by a heavy object, such as a wrecking ball, when it slams into a surface.

IMPLOSION In science, this means the inward collapse of an object from outside pressure. In demolition the destruction of buildings with explosives is called implosion, but the buildings actually collapse from gravity after the explosives have weakened them.

INSULATION MATERIALS In buildings, substances that usually keep heat in and sound out.

LANDFILL SITE A huge hole in the ground where many tons of rubbish are buried and then covered over with soil.

MOMENTUM The speed and weight of an object. The more momentum an object has, the harder it is to stop.

PISTON A cylinder that can be moved up and down inside a tube, to put pressure on a fluid.

PRESSURE The force of something pressing against something else. Even the air exerts a pressure.

REBAR (Short for reinforcing bars) Steel rods used in reinforced concrete to strengthen it.

SAFETY PERIMETER The closest that people are allowed to a dangerous event.

SHOCK WAVE A wave of fast-moving air or liquid.

TARMAC A road surface made of crushed rock and tar.

TOXIC Harmful to living things, including people, animals and plants.

PICTURE CREDITS

(t=top; b=bottom, c=centre; l=left; r=right; f=far)

AFP/Getty 22-23 (main). Alamy 20-21 (main). Brandenburg Industrial Service Company 23bl. Construction Photography 12-13 (main). Corbis 21tc, 24-25 (main), 28-29 (main). Englo 23cfl. Getty Images 8-9 (main), 23cl. Inmalo/MBI 17tl, 17tcr, 17tr. iStockPhoto 11cl, 15cr, 27cr, 28br, 29tr. JCB 1 (main), 2tc, 14-15 (main), 16-17 (foreground main), 18-19 (main), 19bl, 30-31 (main), 30bl, 31 tl. Liebherr obc bl 30tl. New Holland 17tcl. Science Photo Library 10-11 (main), 10-11tl, 23cfr. Shutterstock obc tl, 6-7 (main), 7tl, 9tl, 9c, 11cl, 16-17 (background main) 17c (2 images), 25tl, 26-27 (main), 26tl, 27cl, 27tl, 29cr, 29cl, 30tr, 30br. Ticktock Media Archive 7cl, 7br, 11c (4 images in chart), 12cl, 12bl, 13tl (2 images), 13cr, 15br, 15tl, 15tr, 19tr, 21bl, 23tl, 23tc, 23tr. Uwe Walz/Corbis ofc. Wikimedia 23cr.

Every effort has been made to trace the copyright holders, and we apologize in advance for any unintentional omissions.

We would be pleased to insert the appropriate acknowledgments in any subsequent edition of this publication.